BLOWHOLES BOOK GILLS AND BUTT-BREATHERS

How Animals Get Their Oxygen

DOUG WECHSLER

TILBURY HOUSE PUBLISHERS • THOMASTON, MAINE

For my wife, Debbie Carr, who takes my breath away.

Tilbury House Publishers
Thomaston, Maine 04861
www.tilburyhouse.com

Hardcover ISBN 978-0-88448-772-2
Paperback ISBN 978-0-88448-773-9

Library of Congress Control Number: 2021945810

Cover design by Notch Design
Interior design by Frame25 Productions

Printed in the United States

Acknowledgments

Thanks to Drs. Jessica Dimuzio and Tim Halverson
for comments on the manuscript, and to John
Cann and Craig Latta for photos of the only turtle
known to breathe through its south end.

Photo Credits

Photos are by Doug Wechsler except as follows: page 3 center, RusN / iStock · p.11 sidebar, Doug Perrine/Nature
Picture Library · p.12, Lisa Hoffner/Nature Picture Library · p.12 inset, Tony Heald/Nature Picture Library · p.13
top left, Christophe Courteau/Nature Picture Library · p.13 sidebar right, Klein & Hubert/Nature Picture Library
· p.17 sidebar, Fabio Liverani/Nature Picture Library · p.23 inset, Michael Benard/SmugMug · p.25 sidebar, Bert
Willaert/Nature Picture Library · p.28 main image, Remi Masson/Nature Picture Library · p.29 inset, Remi Masson/
Nature Picture Library · p.29 top, Tim Laman/Nature Picture Library · p.30 inset, Daniel Heuclin/Nature Picture
Library · p.46 both photos, Craig Latta · p.47 inset, Craig Latta · p.47 top, John Cann

O₂, WHAT ARE YOU?

They're headed for your nose!

You can't see them, but they float in the air around you. They invade your body. They stream down your nose and travel through your blood.

What are these invisible invaders? They're oxygen molecules, each one consisting of two atoms of oxygen bonded together. (Atoms of oxygen never travel alone.)

Everything we see is made of molecules, and so are gases we can't see, like oxygen. One molecule is the smallest amount of a substance that can exist. Air is a collection of gas molecules that have no color and no smell. One out of every five gas molecules in air is an oxygen molecule, known as O_2 (OH-TWO) to chemists.

And that's a very good thing for animals like us!

WHO NEEDS O_2?

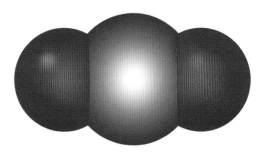

A carbon dioxide molecule is made up of one atom of carbon and two of oxygen.

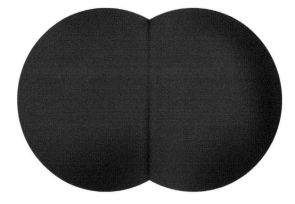

Oxygen atoms pair up to form an oxygen molecule.

You do, for starters.

You are made up of a huge number of cells—brain cells, muscle cells, skin cells, and more—about 30 trillion cells in all, and they all need to be fed. You digest food and send it through your blood stream to cells throughout your body. Your blood also carries oxygen to your cells.

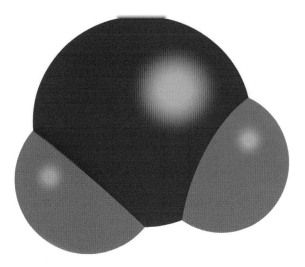

Two hydrogen atoms and one oxygen make a molecule of water, the familiar H_2O.

Inside your cells, oxygen molecules are split into their two component atoms, and each atom combines with digested food to create the energy you need to grow, run, snore, laugh, or do anything else. When their job is done, the oxygen atoms end up in molecules of carbon dioxide (CO_2) and water (H_2O).

We don't want too much carbon dioxide in our bodies, because that would prevent our blood from carrying enough oxygen to the cells where it's needed. So our blood whisks away the carbon dioxide to our lungs, and from there we breathe it out into the air. We inhale to get more oxygen. We exhale to get rid of carbon dioxide. Inhale, exhale. In, out.

Meanwhile, where does the water go? Some will stay in your cells, but most will leave your body in urine or sweat. Some will also go back out through your lungs as water vapor, which is what you see when you breathe on a cold windowpane or mirror.

Orangutans need oxygen. So do owls, oysters, opossums, oakworms, and animals whose names begin with every letter of the alphabet. All animals need oxygen, just like you.

Oakworms, opossums, owls, and oysters need O_2 like you.

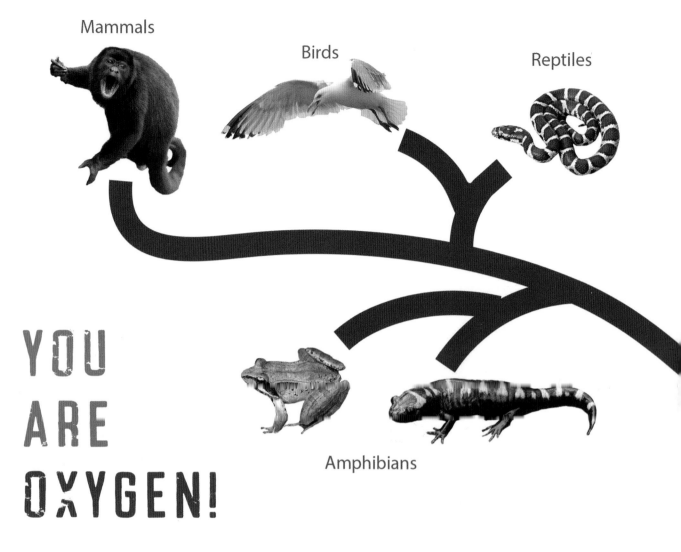

Mammals

Birds

Reptiles

Amphibians

YOU ARE OXYGEN!

Not only do you *need* oxygen, you *are* oxygen. More than half of an average person's weight is oxygen. In large part that is because we are mostly water, and water is mostly oxygen by weight (one oxygen atom and two much lighter hydrogen atoms). Water makes up half to three-quarters of the weight of a human body. Most of the other molecules in our bodies have some oxygen as well. For an animal on planet Earth, there's no getting away from oxygen.

When oxygen molecules enter an animal's cells, they end up in the *mitochondria*, specialized structures that float inside the cell. Each mitochondrion is like a pop-up power-plant. In a complex series of reactions that has been the same in all animals since they evolved 2 billion years ago, mitochondria use oxygen and nutrients to generate energy. Cells that burn loads of energy, such as muscle cells, need loads of mitochondria.

Evolutionary biologists believe that mitochondria started out as tiny single-celled organisms that looked like bacteria. Some of these bacteria-like cells may have become trapped inside cells of more advanced organisms, where—making the best of a bad situation—they created a relationship that benefited both cells. A relationship between two organisms that benefits both is known as a *symbiotic relationship*. Once a relationship like that evolves, neither organism can exist without the other.

Fish

Arthropods

We couldn't live without the mitochondria in our cells, and mitochondria wouldn't survive outside living cells.

Fungi

Plants

Two billion years ago, cells with a nucleus engulfed bacteria that functioned like mitochondria, and the host cells became the ancestors of all life other than bacteria and related microbes.

Cell without mitochondria

Mitochondria-like bacteria

Cell engulfs bacteria

JUST BREATHE

We people are mammals, and most mammals get oxygen pretty much like we do.

Simple, right? Just breathe.

When you breathe in, the *diaphragm* (DIE-ah-fram), a big muscle in your chest just beneath your lungs, pulls down. That causes your rib cage to move up and outward, expanding your chest cavity and relieving the pressure on your lungs. That causes the lungs to expand, drawing air from the outside. The air is sucked into your nose, then flows past the back of your mouth, down your windpipe or *trachea* (TREY-kee-uh), into two tubes called *bronchi* (BRON-keye), and through them to your lungs.

In your lungs, the air fills 400 million tiny chambers called *alveoli* (al-vee-OH-leye).

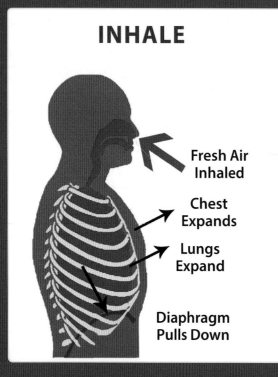

INHALE

Fresh Air
Inhaled

Chest
Expands

Lungs
Expand

Diaphragm
Pulls Down

As we inhale, the diaphragm pulls down and the rib cage expands, reducing pressure on the lungs and allowing them to expand and pull in air.

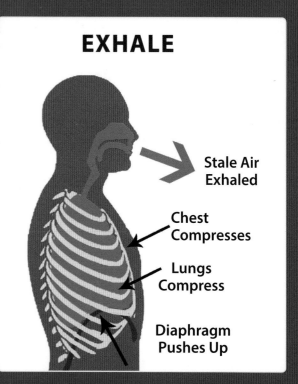

EXHALE

Stale Air
Exhaled

Chest
Compresses

Lungs
Compress

Diaphragm
Pushes Up

When we exhale, the diaphragm pushes up and the rib cage contracts, pushing stale air out of the lungs.

Each chamber is surrounded by blood vessels, and oxygen seeps through the blood-vessel walls. Inside the vessels, red blood cells trap oxygen and take it for a ride into bigger and bigger vessels. It all ends up in two large vessels, the pulmonary veins, that pour the blood into the left side of your heart.

Your heart pumps the oxygenated blood out through arteries that branch into smaller and smaller vessels entering all parts of your body. Cells next to the smallest vessels—the *capillaries*—take up oxygen from the blood and send carbon dioxide into the blood. That carbon dioxide travels in the blood through veins to the right side of your heart. Your heart pumps it through vessels back to your lungs, where it leaves the blood and diffuses into your alveoli.

Now breathe out. Get rid of that carbon dioxide. Phew! Breathe in, breathe out. In, out. Your body knows what to do.

The process of getting oxygen into the body and getting carbon dioxide out is called *respiration*. Other animals respire by breathing in and out just as we do, but not all of them. Many have evolved other ways to respire, and some of those ways are bizarre.

HOW NATURE WORKS

AIR, PLEASE

You may need three times more oxygen while swimming than while resting.

The average person breathes in about 2,900 gallons (11,000 liters) of air each day. About 20 percent of that is oxygen. When we exhale, our breath contains about 15 percent oxygen. The oxygen we use is therefore 5 percent of all the air we inhale—about 145 gallons (550 liters) of oxygen each day. When you exercise heavily, you need much more.

BLOWHOLE BREATH

Whales are mammals too, but they don't breathe the same way other mammals do. Fifty million years ago, whales' ancestors lived on land, had legs, and breathed through nostrils at the ends of their snouts. Like dogs, whale ancestors probably had to raise their heads above water to breathe while swimming. With nostrils like that, a whale would never get much rest in the water. But over the course of several million years of evolution, those nostrils moved to the top of the head, allowing a whale to rest and breathe while floating on the surface.

Whales don't breathe automatically like we do. They have to think about each breath, so when they sleep, only half the brain snoozes.

A pilot whale breathes. Out with the bad air ...

... and in with the good.

Some whales can dive nearly two miles deep and stay underwater for 90 minutes. How can they hold their breath so long? For one thing, when they spout, almost all the air in their lungs shoots out and is replaced with fresh air. Also, pound for pound, whales have a lot more blood than we do, and that extra blood stores and distributes a lot more oxygen to a whale's body, oxygen needed to fuel swimming muscles and keep the brain working. Reserves of oxygen are stored in the muscles by a chemical called *myoglobin*. And when a whale dives, its body shuts off the blood supply to the stomach and other parts that don't need energy right away, preserving more oxygen for the parts that do.

HOW NATURE WORKS

QUIET CHEWERS, NOISY BREATHERS

Whale spouts can top out at an altitude of 40 feet (12 meters).

The passageway from a whale's nostrils does not connect to the mouth like ours does. Whales don't have to worry about getting water in their lungs while they eat. If you were a whale, you couldn't blow bubbles while chewing gum.

Whales are noisy breathers. On a calm day, you can hear a fin whale breathe from a mile away. A whale shoots air out of its blowhole at 150 miles (240 km) per hour; the spout you see is mostly exhaled warm water vapor condensing into droplets as it hits the cooler air. Experienced captains and marine biologists can tell what kind of whale is blowing by the shape of the spout.

A SIZABLE SCHNOZZOLA

Greeting with entwined trunks.

An elephant enjoys a pleasant dirt bath.

Which mammal has the longest nose of all? An elephant, of course. The elephant's 6-foot-long (2 meters) trunk takes elephant-sized breaths. One breath sucks 9 gallons (34 liters) of air into an elephant's lungs. That's 70 times the volume of a human breath.

Elephant lungs are different from most mammals' lungs in that they don't sit in an open cavity, but instead attach directly to the walls of the chest. The chest muscles, rather than a diaphragm, cause the lungs to expand and contract.

An elephant can breathe through its mouth as well as its trunk, leaving that versatile schnozzola available for other tasks.

With built-in snorkels, elephants are great swimmers.

An elephant breathes through its mouth
when its trunk is full of dirt or water.

TRUNK TRICKS

An elephant's trunk comes in handy for more than breathing. Here's what a trunk can do:

- Lift 700 pounds (317 kg).

- Shell a peanut.

- Load up with 8 gallons (30 liters) of water for a drink or a cool bath.

- Spray dirt on its owner's back to combat sunburn and insect bites.

- Grasp bundles of grass.

- Snag tasty leaves as high as 20 feet (6 meters) above the ground.

- Greet another elephant by wrapping around its trunk and into its mouth.

- Help a baby elephant stand after birth.

- Smell water a mile away.

All in all, an elephant's trunk is nothing to sneeze at.

Elephants can reach food at about
the same height as giraffes.

"Hello, my friend."

BIRDS BREATHE IN CIRCLES

A flying bird like this peregrine falcon needs plenty of oxygen.

Birds aren't mammals; they're descended from long-extinct dinosaurs. But they're animals, and that means they need oxygen.

In fact, since birds burn a lot of energy when they fly, they need a *lot* of oxygen. A bird's lungs attach to six or more air sacs. If you could travel inside an air sac, you would be surrounded by what looks like a wet, clear plastic bag. As muscles move a bird's breastbone up and down, air is forced in and out of the air sacs.

Bird lungs are very different from mammal lungs. They are much smaller, and they do not expand and contract. Instead, the air sacs act as bellows, forcing air through the lungs when they contract. Air flows one way through the lungs and out the other side, traveling in a loop inside the bird. The entire trip takes two breaths, as illustrated at right. At step 3, the second inhalation brings in new air that follows the same loop two steps behind the first breath. Compare bird breathing with human breathing. When we breathe out, we can't exhale every bit of air. So each time we inhale, fresh air mixes with a little bit of "stale" air. This never happens in a bird, because the air travels in a loop.

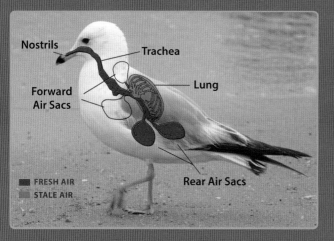

Step 1 of a bird breath gets air through
the nostrils and to the rear air sacs.

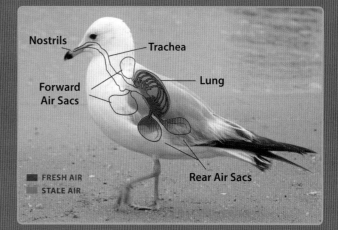

In Step 2, the air is forced into the
lungs, which extract oxygen.

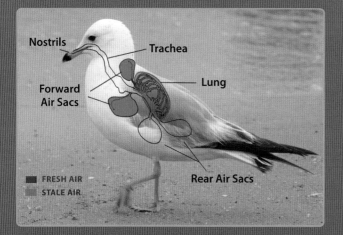

In Step 3, oxygen-depleted air
travels to the forward air sacs.

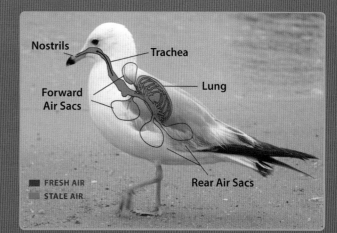

Finally, air is squeezed from the forward
air sacs and exhaled through the nostrils.

HOW NATURE WORKS

HOW HIGH CAN THEY FLY?

Thanks to their efficient breathing, some birds can fly as high as the peak of Mount Everest, the tallest mountain in the world at 29,032 feet (8,849 meters) above sea level. At that altitude there is less than a third as much oxygen as at sea level. Most human climbers need an oxygen tank to survive at that altitude, though a few hardy (foolhardy?) climbers have summited Everest without supplemental oxygen.

THE SKINNY ON SNAKES

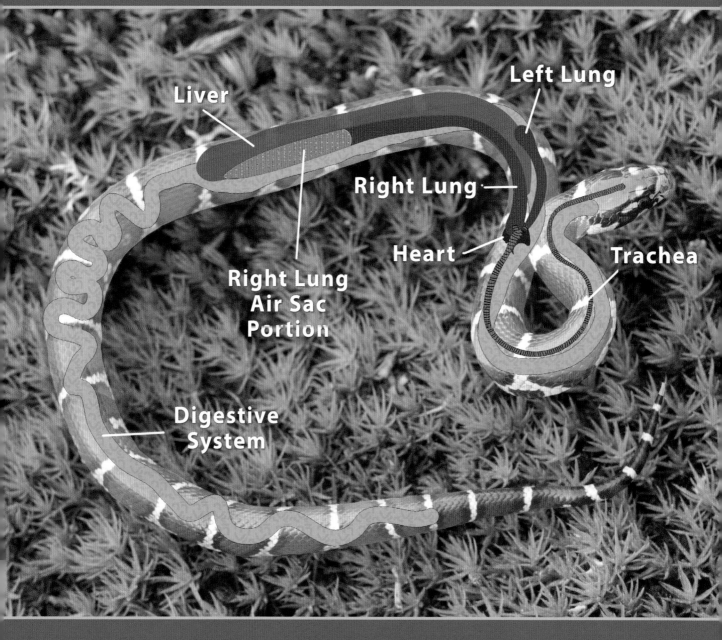

Liver

Left Lung

Right Lung

Right Lung
Air Sac
Portion

Heart

Trachea

Digestive
System

From birds we turn to reptiles—snakes, to be specific. A slender snake has a space problem when it comes to housing organs. Its liver, kidneys, stomach, and lung have to be long and skinny, and most snakes don't have room for two lungs like other reptiles. All snakes have a full-sized right lung, but most have only a tiny left lung or none at all.

When a snake breathes, air enters through the nostrils, then passes through the back of the throat and the windpipe. From there it passes through the bronchus to the right lung, which may be half the length of the snake or longer.

This snake's windpipe, or trachea, is clearly visible just above its tongue.

Oxygen and carbon dioxide are exchanged in the front part of the lung, a honeycomb of folds filled with tiny blood vessels. The rear of the lung is a hollow air sac, not designed to absorb oxygen. But that space is not wasted. The air stored there is useful when the snake needs extra oxygen—for example, when it is fleeing or swimming underwater. Filling the air sac can also make the snake look big and threatening to a predator. Some snakes also use the stored air to hiss, pushing it out through a narrow passageway into the mouth to create the sound.

HOW NATURE WORKS

WHY SNAKES DON'T CHOKE

How does a snake breathe when its mouth is stuffed—say, when it's swallowing a big frog whole? It lowers its jaw and extends its windpipe out of its mouth. Only a snake can do that, and it's a handy trick to have when you're a python swallowing an alligator in the Florida Everglades.

A snake extends its trachea out of its mouth while eating a frog.

AMPHIBIAN AIR PUMPS

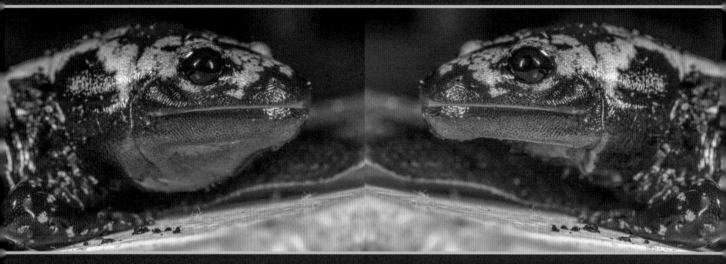

A marbled salamander pumps air in and out of its mouth and lungs by pushing the mouth's floor up and down.

From reptiles we go to amphibians. Watch a salamander or frog, and you will see the skin under its mouth moving up and down. It is pumping air in and out of its lungs.

To inhale, a salamander's throat muscles pull the floor of the mouth down while the mouth remains shut. This sucks air through the nose and into the mouth. Then the salamander closes the nostrils and opens the *glottis* (the gateway to the windpipe). As it raises the floor of its mouth, the air is forced through the windpipe and into the lungs.

To exhale, it reverses these actions, opening the glottis and lowering the floor of the mouth to suck air out of the lungs. Then it closes the glottis, opens the nostrils, and pulls the floor of the mouth up, forcing air out through the nostrils.

A green frog lowers the floor of its mouth with its nostrils open to suck air into its mouth.

Then, with nostrils closed and glottis open, it raises the floor of its mouth, pumping the air from its mouth to its lungs.

GILLS WITH FRILLS

The gills of a tiger salamander larva have many fine branches.

The ancestors of amphibians evolved from fish with lungs about 360 million years ago. Today, most amphibian larvae still start life in water like their fish ancestors.

When marbled salamanders and most other amphibians hatch from eggs underwater, feathery gills stick out from behind their heads like a pair of shrubs. Tiny blood vessels fill the many "twigs," and the branching creates plenty of surface area to absorb oxygen and release carbon dioxide.

Marbled salamanders are adapted to living in wetlands that dry up in summer. Early in the summer, the larvae metamorphose to their adult forms. They grow lungs during this transformation, and the gills break down to be recycled inside the salamander's body.

A marbled salamander larva shows off its feathery gills.

SURFACE AREA: THE KEY TO EFFICIENT RESPIRATION

When oxygen and carbon dioxide diffuse into or out of an organism, the exchange takes place across membranes. The more surface area the membranes have, the more exchange can take place. To maximize surface area, the tissues where animals absorb oxygen are divided into many tiny units. Think of the many branches of a salamander larva's gills, the millions of alveoli in our lungs, or the many tiny blood vessels in a fish's gills. In each case, having many tiny units increases the total surface area for diffusion and therefore the amount of gas exchange that can take place.

To see how surface area increases when you break something into tiny parts, imagine covering the entire outside surface of a loaf of bread with an even layer of peanut butter. Now, cut the loaf in half. You have the same amount of bread, but there are two more surfaces to coat with peanut butter. Now cut each half in two, and you have another four surfaces to coat, and so on. The more units you break something into, the more surface area it will have.

A red-backed salamander breathes through moist skin and the lining of its mouth.

SKINNY SALAMANDERS

Have you seen the most common vertebrate (animal with a backbone) in the forests of the northeastern US? Probably not, unless you have turned over a rock or log to search for it. The red-backed salamander has good reason to hide during the day. It has to keep its skin wet.

This salamander and its close relatives have neither gills nor lungs. Instead, oxygen oozes through their skin and the lining of their mouths. They must remain moist, or gas will not pass through their thin skin. That's why these salamanders only venture out on humid nights.

Red-backed salamanders lay their eggs inside moist rotten logs or underground. The female guards the eggs until they hatch six weeks later. Inside the eggs, the embryos grow gills to get oxygen from the moist surroundings. Just after hatching, the nearly inch-long (2 cm) hatchlings lose their gills and breathe through their skin.

A red-backed salamander guards its eggs in a moist underground retreat that has been exposed for this photo.

ANOTHER WRINKLE ON BREATHING

One of the ugliest frogs in the world is also one of the strangest. It lives high in the Andes Mountains of South America—12,500 feet (3,800 meters) above sea level—in Lake Titicaca. The atmosphere at that altitude has only 60 percent of the oxygen it contains at sea level.

Unlike most frogs, the Lake Titicaca frog spends its entire life underwater, and that water is cold! Fortunately for the frog, cold water holds more oxygen than warm water. The frog has small lungs but makes up for that with its very loose, folded skin. The many folds create a lot of surface area for oxygen to enter through, and tiny blood vessels near the skin surface take up that oxygen.

Several adaptations allow the Titicaca frog to live its submarine life. It is sluggish, so it doesn't need as much oxygen as a more active animal. (Think how much heavier you breathe when you run.) Also, it has the smallest red blood cells of any frog, and these take up oxygen faster than larger cells. And its blood can carry more oxygen than other frogs' blood can.

If the frog gets into water with low oxygen, it will rise so that only its nostrils break the surface of the water. It can then breathe with its small lungs. If it can't reach the water surface, it will stand on its toes and bob up and down, flapping its skin folds. This moves more water and therefore more oxygen over the skin.

Skin wrinkles create more surface area for oxygen to enter the body of a Titicaca frog.

24

UGLY FROG FACES UGLY FATE

In 1968, famous underwater explorer Jacque Cousteau searched the bottom of Lake Titicaca for a legendary lost city. He didn't find the city, but he did marvel at the abundance of giant frogs.

Now the Lake Titicaca frog is an endangered species. Because most amphibians get some or nearly all of their oxygen through their skin, they are particularly vulnerable to pollution. Agriculture and human settlements around Titicaca's shores release pollutants into the lake. Just as oxygen readily diffuses through the frog's thin skin, so do pollutants. Fertilizer run-off also causes bacteria to grow and use up oxygen in the lake.

And the frogs face another threat, too: People eat them raw, blended with herbs and honey as a medicine.

A BREATH OF
FISH AIR

For more active underwater animals, breathing is a whole other kettle of fish. There is much more oxygen gas in air than in water.

Water streams in through the paddlefish's mouth, over the gills, and out through the gill slit.

One cup of air has as much oxygen as 30 cups of water. So how do fish get the oxygen they need? Whales and other marine mammals have to surface to breathe, but fish breathe underwater. How do they do it?

They use gills. There is a curved flap behind a fish's head that opens and closes, and inside that slit are four dark-red, fan-shaped gills. Each fan is divided into many strips, like the teeth of a comb, and each strip has many ridges full of tiny blood vessels. Tuna, the racing boats of the fish world, may have seven million of these teeny ridges on their gills. Water flows through the fish's mouth and over the gills. Oxygen seeps from the water into the tiny blood vessels. Carbon dioxide seeps out. The blood travels to the heart, and oxygen is pumped around the body.

The paddlefish's gills, seen through the gill slit, are red because they are packed with tiny blood vessels.

HOW NATURE WORKS

WHY FISH LIKE WATER

Water with carbon dioxide waste exits through the large gill slit behind this rockfish's head.

Why can't most fish breathe out of water? Think about it this way: If you swim underwater, your hair spreads out. When you come out of the pool, it mats down on your head. The same thing happens to a fish's gills. Underwater, the parts of the gills separate, exposing all their surfaces for use. But the gills stick together out of water, and oxygenated water can't flow over and between them.

A FISH OUT OF WATER

The tide goes out on a tropical mangrove swamp, leaving the mudflat dry. A comical-looking, bug-eyed fish called a mudskipper walks on the mudflat. This fish out of water has no trouble breathing. Its skin, mouth, and throat have lots of blood vessels to absorb oxygen. It can live for days on land, as long as it stays wet. When it reaches a wet spot in the mud, it quickly rolls over to moisten its skin.

Mudskippers build burrows in the wet mud. The female lays eggs in the burrow, and the male takes care of them. The burrow is U-shaped and closed on one end.

Male mudskippers face off on a mudflat.

To replenish the oxygen that the eggs need, the male gulps air and swims down the burrow and up into the other leg of the U. When he opens his mouth, a bubble floats up into the eggs.

Unlike any other fish, male mudskippers feed, court females, and defend their territories out of water. In fact, some mudskippers would die if they had to stay underwater for long. Their small gills do not absorb enough oxygen from the water.

Mudskippers can live longer out of water than in it.

A mudskipper burrows in a tidal mudflat.

WHAT TO CALL A WALKING FISH?

Mudskippers get their name from their unusual means of locomotion. They use their fins to do a sort of breaststroke on the mud. The jerky motion is a little like skipping.

AMPHIBIAN WANNABE

African lungfish start life with gills but soon develop lungs to breathe air.

A man digs a lungfish out of its cocoon in Togo, Africa.

As you might guess from the name, African lungfish breathe through lungs. They also have gills, but their gills are too small to gather sufficient oxygen for the fish to survive for long underwater. Lungfish must come to the surface to gulp air, just like marine mammals. The lungs connect directly, just behind the mouth, without a windpipe. Inside a lung, many tiny chambers with blood vessels absorb oxygen.

It burrows down into the mud of a drying stream or pond and snuggles into a small chamber, covering the walls with slimy mucus, which dries to form a cocoon. The lungfish remains in the cocoon, breathing air until rains fill the stream again. The fish doesn't move during this time; its breathing slows down, and its muscles break down to provide nutrients for the rest of the body. The lungfish can stay alive up to a year in its cocoon. It isn't luxury, but it's a living.

A FISH HAS TO BREATHE!

Fish have evolved many other ways to get oxygen. Here are a few variations:

◆ When out of water, the African snakehead uses an air-filled chamber behind the gills. The chamber is crowded with blood vessels to soak up oxygen from the air.

◆ The electric eel lives in muddy waters that may have little oxygen, so it must surface to breathe. It gulps air and absorbs oxygen though the highly folded, bumpy surfaces of its mouth.

◆ A number of catfishes can breathe by swallowing air and absorbing it through the intestine wall.

◆ American eels get some of their oxygen through their skin.

Electric eel.

African snakehead.

American eel.

BOOK GILLS

So far we've been looking at ways of breathing in vertebrate animals (animals with backbones). But up to 97 percent of all animal species are invertebrates (without backbones), and what an amazing variety of breathing styles they've developed! Take book gills, for example . . . .

Book gills must work pretty well, because horseshoe crabs have been breathing with them for 450 million years. There is no other animal like a horseshoe crab, so maybe it's not surprising that no other living animal breathes like a horseshoe crab.

Five pairs of book gills hide behind a series of leathery plates on the underside of a horseshoe crab, each gill containing more than twice the number of pages in this book. The "pages" are folds of gill tissue, each fold loaded with blood vessels to absorb oxygen from the seawater that flows around it. The oxygenated blood then flows to the heart and is pumped around the body.

The underside of a horseshoe crab shows the leathery plates that protect the book gills.

"Living fossils," horseshoe crabs were already breathing with book gills 200 million years before the first dinosaur was born.

In spring, horseshoe crabs crawl up on the beach to spawn. They may spend half a day stranded above the water until the tide comes back. Fortunately, book gills work out of water as long as they stay wet—unlike the softer, less rigid gills of fishes. The horseshoe crabs stay half-buried in wet sand, waiting for the next high tide.

Horseshoe crabs spawning on a beach at high tide.

A TRUE "BLUE BLOOD"

Horseshoe crab blood is blue thanks to copper in the oxygen-carrying molecules in the blood cells. (Mammals combine oxygen with iron rather than copper, which is why human blood is red.) Horseshoe crab blood is unusual in another way too: It contains a substance (Limulus amebocyte lysate) that can be used to ensure the sterility of medical equipment and injectable drugs. If you've ever had an injection, vaccination, or surgery, you've benefited from horseshoe crab blood!

A SIMPLE SYSTEM

Jellyfish are not actually fish—they belong to the phylum Cnidaria—and are more properly known as sea jellies, just as starfish are more properly called sea stars. Sea jellies don't bother with lungs or gills, and they don't have blood vessels to carry oxygen around their bodies. Still, their cells need oxygen just like all living cells. How do they get it?

The entire surface area of a sea jelly, both outside and inside, absorbs oxygen from the water.

A sea jelly is like a jelly sandwich—two layers of tissue separated by a whole bunch of jelly. The outside layer of living cells is the first thing you see; this is the *epidermis*. To see the inside layer, you'd have to peer in through the sea jelly's mouth (which is also its anus, by the way) into an open space filled with water. This is the *gastric cavity*, the sea jelly's stomach, and its lining is a layer of cells called the *gastrodermis*.

The big space between the epidermis and the gastrodermis is filled with jelly, and because the cells of both dermal layers are always in contact with water, oxygen can seep directly into them.

The jelly is mostly water, with just enough fibers to give the animal its shape as long as it stays in water. Jelly can store oxygen, and this allows sea jellies to survive in polluted waters with little oxygen. Woe to the sea jelly that gets stranded on a beach, however. Evaporation shrinks it as fast as water shrank the Wicked Witch of the West in *The Wizard of Oz*.

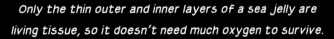

Only the thin outer and inner layers of a sea jelly are living tissue, so it doesn't need much oxygen to survive.

BUG BREATH

The Miracle of the Spiracle

A beetle's tiny spiracles are located on the sides of the abdomen.

The little black Os on the sides of a red-humped caterpillar could stand for oxygen, but really they are spiracles, the gateways to the caterpillar's breathing system. They open and close to let air in and keep water out.

Caterpillars and other insects don't have noses, lungs, or gills, and their "skin" is actually an exoskeleton that doesn't allow much oxygen to pass into the body. That's where the little black Os come in.

The spiracles open to a network of branching tubes that fork into smaller and smaller passageways inside the body. The ends of the tiniest branches have openings to usher air to cells all around the body.

Oxygen diffuses into the cells, and carbon dioxide seeps out of the cells and passes through the tubes and out through the spiracles.

In more active insects like honeybees and sphinx moths, there are air sacs in the middle of the tube network. The flying insect's muscles squeeze and relax like bellows, forcing air in and out of the air sacs and pushing it through the tube system. This pump speeds delivery of fresh air to the cells so that busy bees and moths have energy for flight and foraging.

Flight muscles of the snowberry clearwing moth pump air in and out of the moth's body.

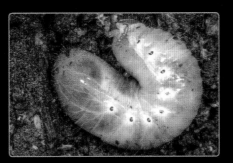

White tubes radiating from orange spiracles in this beetle grub, easy to see toward its rear end, carry oxygen into the body and pass carbon dioxide out.

The round, black spiracles open to a system of tubes carrying air to all parts of the red-humped caterpillar's body.

AQUATIC INSECTS

Three large gills at the rear of a damselfly nymph capture oxygen from the water.

Hold your breath as we dive beneath the surface to see how insects breathe underwater. Because the amount of oxygen in water is tiny compared with the same volume of air, aquatic insects need a way to collect whatever they can get. Look at the rear end of a damselfly nymph and you will see what look like three banners coming out of the backside. These are gills.

Damselfly nymphs don't have spiracles. Instead, oxygen must seep through the thin gill surfaces. The gills have to be large so that they can capture sufficient oxygen.

Just below the surface of these gills is an extensive series of tubes that resemble a tree without leaves. These hollow "twigs" fan out across the gill and absorb oxygen through the thin gill covering. Oxygen goes from the twigs into the "trunk" and then into the abdomen of the nymph. From there, branching tubes carry air to all parts of the body, as in land-dwelling insects.

Damselfly nymph gills do double duty. They also act as paddles, helping to propel the nymphs through the water.

Tubes in the gills carry oxygen to the body.

GILL PADDLES

Mayfly nymphs respire much like damselfly nymphs. The leaf-shaped gills on their back wave in the water, taking in oxygen to a similar system of tubes.

BUTT-BREATHER

We humans prefer to breathe through our noses and mouths. But dragonfly nymphs—the immature dragonflies that live underwater—breathe though the other end. Muscles in their abdomen relax, expanding the space inside their abdomen, sucking water in through the anus.

Once inside, water passes over the gills, which are located inside the rectum at the tail end of the digestive system. The gills have lots of folds, so there is plenty of surface area to soak up the oxygen. The insides of the gills connect to a tube system that carries oxygen to the cells. As the nymph contracts its muscles, the water shoots back out the butt, carrying carbon dioxide.

You might think that combining pooping with breathing would pollute the nymph's gills. Fortunately, by the time food waste reaches a nymph's rectum, it is neatly packaged into little pellets, which the nymph shoots out with a jet of water.

A dragonfly molting from an aquatic butt-breather to an airborne insect that breathes through spiracles on its sides.

Dragonfly nymphs breathe
through their rear ends.

If the nymph senses danger, it shoots water out of the anus with great force, propelling it forward to escape. This rocket propulsion also speeds up respiration, providing the nymph with the extra oxygen and energy it needs to move quickly. So hats off to this butt-breather. An anus that can breathe, eliminate waste, and power an escape is a talented anus.

HOW NATURE
WORKS

OBSERVING THE DRAGONFLY JETSTREAM

Water (with a dye added) shoots out the rear
of a dragonfly nymph, carrying excess CO_2.

Drag a dipnet through vegetation in a healthy pond, and you can usually catch a dragonfly nymph. Hold it on the sides and it may shoot a stream of water. Be gentle with it; it won't bite you.

SNORKEL SNIFFER

Breathing while submerged in sludge can be tough, but one maggot, the hoverfly larva, has a nice solution to this problem. It grows a breathing tube—a snorkel, or siphon—from its rear end. The tube is usually about as long as the maggot but can stretch to six times as long, reaching to the sludge surface to bring in air to a spiracle on the maggot's butt. Because the tube looks like a tail, this larva is known as a rat-tailed maggot.

Rat-tailed maggots often live in stinky places like sewage lagoons and manure ponds. Bacteria eating poop in these ponds use up most of the oxygen, so aquatic insects with gills cannot live there, but the living is easy for a maggot with a butt snorkel.

A hoverfly larva's siphon can extend several body lengths to the surface of the water to get air.

FROM SEWER TO GARDEN

When the rat-tailed maggot becomes an adult hoverfly, it breathes like most other insects, through spiracles on its sides. It also lives in pleasanter environments, like your garden, and visits flowers. Next time you see one on a blossom, imagine where it has been!

BUBBLE BREATHER

A bubble is the dingy diver water beetle's scuba tank.

Like a scuba diver, the water beetle known as the dingy diver carries a tank of air underwater. To gather this air, the beetle bobs its butt above the surface so that a group of tiny hairs can trap a bubble onto the rear. The air in the bubble connects to spiracles on the butt, so the beetle breathes the same way land-dwelling insects do.

The dingy diver has one advantage over scuba divers. As it depletes oxygen from the bubble, more oxygen seeps into the bubble from the water. This resupply only lasts so long, however. Slowly the bubble shrinks, and eventually the beetle must return to the surface for another bubble.

HOW NATURE WORKS

HIDDEN AIR TANKS

Other diving beetles, backswimmers, and water bugs also scuba dive. Their bubble air tanks nestle below the wings instead of clinging to the rear end.

A backswimmer swims upside down, breathing from a bubble beneath its wings.

The diving beetle carries air beneath its hard upper wings, which are called elytra.

BUTT-BREATHING TURTLE

A Fitzroy River turtle crawls on shore, breathing with its lungs like other turtles.

Underwater, a Fitzroy River turtle takes 15 to 60 breaths per minute through its anus.

Speaking of butt-breathers—and since we're coming to the tail end of this journey—let's return to the vertebrate world and what may just be the strangest butt-breather of all.

Australians call the wilds of their country the Outback, and you can find some pretty odd animals there, one being the Fitzroy River turtle. This turtle breathes in and out of its butt, inside of which is a space called the *cloaca*, which is the last stop for poop, pee, and eggs before they leave the turtle's body through the anus. The turtle's cloaca has two side pockets called *bursae* (BUR-see), which are surrounded by tiny blood vessels.

This "bum-breather" rarely leaves the water.

Water streams in and out of the turtle's cloaca and bursae, bringing oxygen to the blood vessels and removing carbon dioxide. The bursae work much like the lungs and gills of other animals.

The locals call this turtle a "bum-breather," and it can stay underwater for days. It also has a perfectly good pair of lungs, however, and has no problem breathing out of water. The Fitzroy River turtle is the only butt-breathing turtle discovered so far.

HOW NATURE WORKS

A SCIENTIST'S VIEW

The world's only known bum-breathing turtle lives in a single river basin in a small part of Australia.

Scientists measured and looked deeply into the rear end of the bum-breather. The anal opening is just over an inch across (30 millimeters). In bright sunlight it is possible to see four inches (100 mm) into the turtle's cloaca, where the blood vessel – lined bursae exchange respiratory gases. The turtle pumps water in and out of the bursae at 15 to 60 times a minute.

O2, THANK YOU!

Whether we breathe with lungs, gills, spiracles, skin, or our butts, we animals would not be here without oxygen. Billions of people breathe in O_2 and exhale CO_2 and H_2O. So do trillions of other animals. How come we don't run out of oxygen?

Here's why: Green plants use CO_2, H_2O, and the energy of sunlight to create sugar. This is called photosynthesis. While producing sugar, oxygen is left over. So the O_2 is recycled back into the air. We owe our lives to plants and the oxygen they produce. Thank you, spinach, grass, trees, phytoplankton, and all your photosynthesizing relatives!

Plants and animals could not live without each other. We animals produce too much carbon dioxide, and plants produce excess oxygen. It's the ultimate symbiotic relationship!

ADDITIONAL RESOURCES

Online

www.brown.edu/Departments/Engineering/Courses/En123/MuscleExp/Frog%20Respiration.htm
An overview of frog respiration.

https://kidshealth.org/en/kids/lungs.html
How people breathe.

www.slate.com/blogs/wild_things/2015/11/17/animal_respiration_walrus_frog_and_butt_breathing_turtle.html
More on some of the stranger aspects of animal respiration.

www.shmoop.com/animal-movement/animal-respiration.html
A good overview of animal respiration.

Books

Orr, Tamra, *Super Cool Science Experiments: Respiration* (Science Explorer). Cherry Lake Publishing, 2009.

Simon, Seymour, *Lungs: All about Our Respiratory System and More!* Collins, 2007.

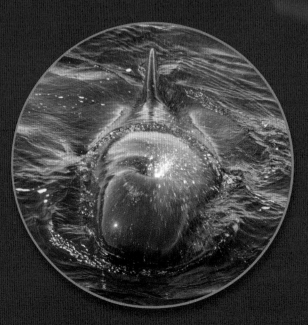

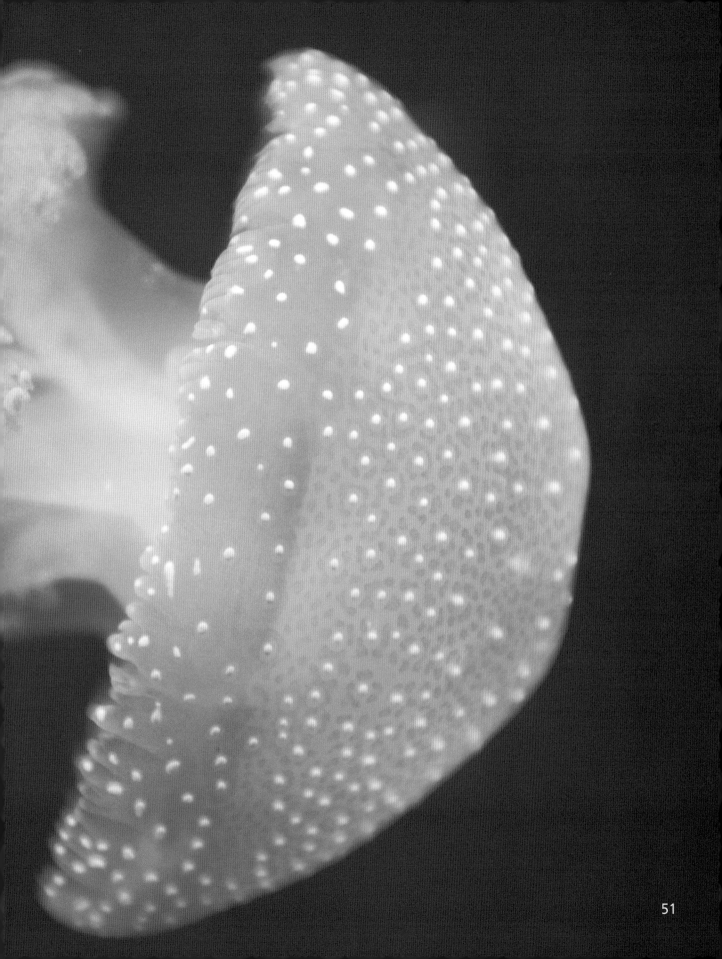

GLOSSARY

air sac: A hollow pouch connected to the lung (in birds) or a part of the lung (in snakes) that provides extra storage space for incoming air.

amphibian: A group of animals (including frogs and salamanders) that usually spend their early lives in water and later move to land.

blowhole: The opening to a whale's nostrils, located on top of the whale's head.

bronchus: The tube leading from the trachea to the lungs in humans and other mammals; plural: bronchi.

bursae: Sacs that open to the cloaca of a bum-breathing turtle and function like the lungs or gills of other animals; singular: bursa.

capillaries: The smallest blood vessels, only slightly wider than the diameter of a blood cell.

carbon dioxide: a gas that combines one carbon atom with two oxygen atoms; scientific formula: CO_2.

cloaca: The chamber at the end of the digestive, reproductive, and urinary systems of reptiles and amphibians.

diaphragm: The muscle in a person's chest that expands and contracts to initiate respiration, causing the lungs to draw in or expel air.

diffuse: To spread freely.

evolve: To change over time from one form into another.

exhale: To breathe out.

exoskeleton: The tough outer armor that covers an insect like skin.

gastric cavity: The hollow, water-filled inner portion of a sea jelly that connects to the surrounding water through the mouth.

gills: Feathery body parts that absorb oxygen from the water into the bloodstream of an aquatic animal.

glottis: The opening to the trachea inside the mouth of amphibians and other vertebrates.

inhale: To breathe in.

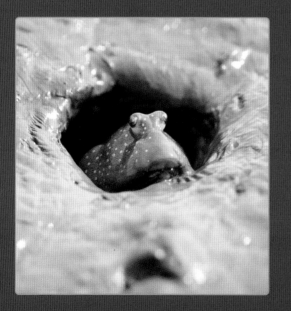

mammal: A group of animals with backbones and hair. Mammals usually give birth to live young and feed their babies milk.

mangrove: A tropical saltwater wetland characterized by mangrove trees and mudflats.

metamorphosis: The change from one life stage to another.

molecule: The smallest unit of a substance or element.

mudflat: A nearly flat muddy area covered by the sea at high tide and exposed at low tide.

myoglobin: A protein in muscles that stores oxygen.

oxygen: The gas in air and water that ani-mals need to breathe; scientific formula: O_2.

photosynthesis: The process by which green plants use energy of sunlight to make sugar from carbon dioxide and water.

predator: An animal that eats other animals.

respiration: The process of breathing in and out to bring oxygen to the cells and carry away carbon dioxide and water.

schnozzola (slang): A big nose. (also, schnozz)

spiracle: A breathing hole in an insect's body.

spout: The jet of water and water vapor that shoots up from a whale's blowhole when the animal forcibly exhales.

trachea: The tube in air-breathing vertebrates that carries air to the lungs; the windpipe. Also: a tube inside insects used in respiration.

vertebrate: A member of a group of animals with backbones, including fish, amphibians, reptiles, birds, and mammals.

windpipe: See trachea.

Doug Wechsler once spent six months in the Brazilian Amazon and has photographed birds in tropical forests around the world. For twenty-eight years he curated the largest collection of bird photographs in the world for the Academy of Natural Sciences of Drexel University, where he is currently Research Associate. He and his wife, Debbie, have volunteered for the Jocotoco Conservation Fund in Ecuador. His twenty-five books for young readers include *The Cicadas Are Coming, The Hidden Life of a Toad*, and *Marvels in the Muck*.